MENTAL ARCHAEOLOGY

Also by Richard Stevko:

Visual-Literary
ABSURDITIES
ABSURDITIES II
THE GHOST TREE – in collaboration with Tamara Stevko

Anapoetry - based upon poetry
CONTRASTS
WHERE THOUGHTS COME FROM
BEYOND A PERSIMMON
TURNABOUTS
ANAPOETRY

Mental Archaeology - formerly known as philosophy
SHADES OF MEANING
MENTAL FUNCTIONING
NEUROPHYSIOLOGY
BEFORE PHILOSOPHY
ORIGINS OF SECRET SOCIETIES
WHO ARE YOU?
THE END OF PHILOSOPHY

Memorial
TASTE OF THE TATRAS

MENTAL ARCHAEOLOGY

Richard Stevko

The Graven Image, Publishing
Hampden, Massachusetts

First Printing

ISBN: 978-1-365-93302-8
Publishing Company: The Graven Image Publishing
Technology Company: Lulu

Freud was engaged in an archaeology of his own, digging into minds to uncover hidden experiences, fragments of past lives that he tried to put again into a living context.

Freud Museum London

Contents

In writing pieces of a certain sort, *Shades of Meaning, Mental Functioning, Neurophysiology* and *Before Philosophy*, the overarching problem of how to categorize the books vexed me. *Neurophysiology* was clearly a text on how the brain works, but its subtitle: *The Biological Basis of Mental Life*, hinted at a broader range than material neurology. The other three were published under the category of Philosophy, where they clearly did not fit comfortably. Every philosopher to whom I showed it, has reacted politely, then clearly objected to the science in it. Obversely, every scientist is at first civil, then intolerant of the subjectivity, the perceived Philosophy in it. Though not a Philosopher, I am a sentient being, and attempt to justify the content, not so much as philosophy, but more as an evaluation of philosophic methodology.

While trying to describe the topics to family, friends and colleagues, I often found myself saying that I wrote about things I dug up out of the depths of my mind; and opted for a while to create the category, "Mental Archeology". While that was descriptive in the vernacular, it implied history that wasn't there (except to some degree in *Before Philosophy*). Archaeology, as an academic discipline, is concerned with the study of antiquity (Archeo-), largely through its physical remnants (ostensibly demonstrating history that _was_ there). It does not traditionally admit endeavors, into its self-described discipline, that do not discover artifacts. Its methods have been maintained though it has begun to root into geography (Assyrian Archaeology) and culture (Feminist Archaeology, Marxist Archaeology). These all still rely on traditional artifacts, although the last two sound like they are relying on subjective data (cultural artifacts, the accrual of which could be construed as soft data - newspapers, social statistical data, etc.).

People who have been noted for exploring the workings of the mind tended to work in fields like psychology, writing, arts, philosophy, medicine and clergy. They have not always flourished in those endeavors because of social pressures on an individual level ranging from very personal, like parents guiding offspring towards gainful employment; to authorities, like the scientists and philosophers mentioned two paragraphs back, who offer "clarity" in their areas; to broad social forces, such as the Behaviorist movement in psychology which actively suppresses introspection. These broadest forces usually have reliable reasons for pushing their agendas, but little investment in exploring views which are superficially contrary, but in depth analysis often seek the same goals. This subtle opposition takes on additional fervor in religion and politics.

Archaeologists in the field have no difficulty describing their endeavor. The lexical definition is clear: "Archaeology is the study of the ancient and recent human past through material remains."[Society for American Archaeology] The common use of the word has evolved an elusive meaning; a vernacular definition could be "digging up old stuff to see how people lived."

Mental Archaeology is, in this writing, a term coined to describe the process by which the author attempts to glean artifacts from the memory, which had been created not by the interaction of objects in the environment, but by subjective interactions of phenomena in the mind. That implies, in this use, that all objective data from the environment have been made available to consciousness as memory, and as whatever influences upon perception that memory has construed.This articulation is broadly used as a metaphor for ineffable endeavors and has been suggested by many (see *Clean-Hand Archaeology*, below) who have expanded their areas of endeavor in creative ways.

Mental Archaeology

is an oxymoron; *mental* refers to abstract concepts and *archaeology* is based on concrete artifacts. Although the term seems incongruous, an empirical model of uncovering layers of abstract modular structures, such as the mind, seems, in a Kantian sense, more genuine than the traditional dialectical method of philosophy. The appeal of archaeology as a metaphor for discovery persists despite academic defense of its lexical declaration. Further evaluation of the history of archaeology, its methodology and current use may be informative.

History of Archaeology

Archaeology, long before becoming a legitimate science in search of knowledge, had its roots in political and religious motivations.
EGYPT - Around 1500 BC, the Egyptians dug up and restored the Sphinx. It had been built almost a millennium earlier and was buried in sand up to its neck.
BABYLON - The next purported excavation was in Babylon by the last Babylonian king, Nabonidus, to restore the temple dedicated to Naram-Sin, the grandson of Sargon, founder of the Dynasty of Akkad, almost 1800 years earlier. Many of the excavations after that could best be described as treasure hunts.
HERCULANEUM AND POMPEII, - Charles of Bourbon in 1738, hired Marcello Venuti to supervise the excavations of Herculaneum and Pompeii, much of which had already been destroyed by fortune hunters.
[Binford]

MODERN - It took many more years, the Enlightenment, and Darwin's work on evolution before Archaeology turned from a treasure hunt to a rigorous discipline with controlled methodology and organized body of knowledge upon which scholars could rely. This continued support of the endeavor as an empirical science gradually lost its rigid and exclusive meaning, when the dirt diggers began to get inundated with new blood; and whether the subsequent changes reflected the incursion of new thinking (the young turks began internal upheaval), the natural evolution of a maturing science, or other disciplines encroaching on the romantic notions emanated from discoveries of the recently formulated and popularized endeavor. After all, who could resist the self image of doing one's tedious work in an exotic locale, wearing a safari jacket and pith helmet. NEW LAYERS OF ARCHAEOLOGY - The Antiquarians were challenged by more socially minded colleagues and Neo-evolutionism, Marxist Archaeology, and Conjunctive Archaeology influenced the ideology of the discipline. Processual Archaeology tried to maintain the integrity of reliance on artifacts, while Behavioral Archaeology and Post-processual Archaeology continued stirring the archaeological pot as other influences pressed. Feminist Archaeology and Urban Archaeology attempted to maintain classical stringent standards, while speculations like *Chariots of the Gods* were shunned as pseudo-archaeology. In the meantime in other reaches of cognitive space, other people, who admired the work archaeologists did, and used the discipline as a metaphor for the space in which they worked, Sigmund Freud and Carl Gustav Jung continued to speculate on the meaning of intangible artifacts they dug up out of their patient's past

Artifacts

Artifacts are man made objects
Origin - from Latin *arte* 'by or using art' + *factum* 'something made'
First Known Use: 1821; Archaeological application dates from 1890.
Two of the earliest uses of the word *artifact* were 1) in archaeology where they are considered to be an object made by a human being, typically an item of cultural or historical interest; and 2) something observed in a scientific investigation or experiment that is not naturally present but occurs as a result of the preparative or investigative procedure.

The first noted use seems to have a positive implication, being an object sought after;
the second noted used has a negative, or artificial connotation being an undesired byproduct of a technique. It would seem that this is the original meaning of the words of similar derivation, like artifice and artificial:
- Definition of *artifice* (noun) in English
  - [O.E.D] Clever or cunning devices or expedients, especially as used to trick or deceive others.
  - [Ety.] 1530s, "workmanship, the making of anything by craft or skill," Meaning "device, trick" (the usual modern sense) is from 1650s.
- Definition of *artificial* (adjective) in English
  - [O.E.D] Made or produced by human beings rather than occurring naturally, typically as a copy of something natural.
  - [Ety.] Meaning "made by man" (opposite of *natural*) is from early 15c.

Though the academic community seems united in accepting the following definitions:

• artifacts - man made objects.
• methodology[1] - including uncovering stratified layers of debris containing artifacts.
• synthesis [Archaeology Wordsmith © 2002-2015] - the assemblage and analysis of data before interpretation.

---

[1] The stratified layers in which artifacts are found represent time layering to an archaeologist, and the method of dating the artifacts begins with careful notation of the location of the objects.

Clean-Hand Archaeology

The intangible aspects of pragmatic archaeology (e.g., methodology, synthesis of information) served many data collectors as a paradigm suitable to the formation of their nascent disciplines or as functional analogies of their incipient techniques.

- Freud, Sigmund (1856 – 1939) - "used archaeological excavation as a metaphor for the remembering of previous experiences in therapy." [Larsen] "In clinical work Freud was engaged in an archaeology of his own, digging into minds to uncover hidden experiences, fragments of past lives that he tried to put again into a living context. Like the archaeologist, the psychoanalyst had to work slowly, with great care, gradually uncovering buried 'objects' and reconstructing the relations between them. And in both professions there are long periods of frustration followed by periods of elation and excitement. So like archaeology, psychoanalysis dealt with *uncovering the past*, with *fragments*, and with *interpretation* or reconstruction." [Freud Museum London]

- Jung, Carl Gustav (1875 – 1961) linked the collective unconscious to "what Freud called *archaic remnants* - mental forms whose presence cannot be explained by anything in the individual's own life and which seem to be aboriginal, innate, and inherited shapes of the human mind". [Jung]

- Benjamin, Walter (1892 – 1940) - "Language has unmistakably made plain that memory is not an instrument for exploring the past, but rather a medium. It is the medium of that which is experienced, just as the earth is the medium in which ancient cities lie buried. He who seeks to approach his own buried past must conduct himself like a man digging." [Benjamin]

- Riegl, Alois (1858 – 1905) - developed the idea of a *Kunstwollen*[2] "Art expresses the way man wants to see things shaped or colored, just as the poetic *Kunstwollen* expresses the way man wants to imagine them." [C.S. Wood] As such, each artist participates in each act of creation as a representative of that particular interaction with the environment. This debate continues, but Riegl, following Nietzsche, and followed by Rank, instantiated the idea that aesthetics imbued in all crafts and cultural poetics steeped the very interaction of man with nature. Indeed, he implied the history of western art was a *contest* [Riegl] *with nature*.
- Foucault, Michel (1926 – 1984) - Archaeology plus genealogy became essential methods for Foucault because archaeology provided a method that did not rely primarily on the individual subject's consciousness as in phenomenology and in traditional historiography. The genealogical technique introduced tiers of discursive observers to counter the effect of contingency enmeshed in different points of view. [Gutting]
- Neo-evolutionism (1930s) is a social theory based on empirical evidence from fields such as archeology, paleontology, and historiography. It tries to explain the evolution of societies by drawing on

---

2 translated as (*will to art, inspiration?*). represented as 1) a refutation that art is a skill in representing nature; that expertise contingent on historical factors. 2) an affirmation that art is an inspiration at each age and in each culture to willingly interpret the world in their own way.

Charles Darwin's (1809 – 1882) theory of evolution and discarding some dogmas of the previous social evolutionism. Proponents say Neo-evolutionism is objective and simply descriptive, eliminating any references to a moral or cultural system of values.

• Panksepp, Jaak(1943 -) has spent his career studying the primary emotional processes that have their origins in the ancient parts of the brain and are shared by all mammals. In his latest framing [Panksepp] he takes an evolutionary approach to understanding their development.

As these scientists found that the methodology of Archaeology better suited their respective explorations they appropriated the title of the group (Archaeology) who developed that methodology. Conversely, Francisco Varela attempted to develop a rigorous method and an explicit pragmatics for exploration and analysis of the field of conscious phenomena.[Varella] He found a method, called phenomenology, that had originated "in the 20th century, the primary objective of which is the direct investigation and description of phenomena as consciously experienced, without theories about their causal explanation and as free as possible from unexamined preconceptions and presuppositions."[Spiegelberg]

The discipline of phenomenology[3]

definition:
- Initially - the study of structures of experience, or consciousness.
- Literally - the study of "phenomena":
  appearances of things
  or things as they appear in our experience
  or the ways we experience things,
    thus the meanings things have in our experience.

Phenomenology studies conscious experience as experienced from the subjective or first person point of view. Science is usually considered more reliable because its methods are objective. However, in the empirical endeavors, this did not seem important as long as the observers remained objective as well. Following the enlightenment the facade began to crumble. In the quantum age, the issue was totally exposed when Heisenberg postulated his uncertainty principle and the interaction between objectivity and subjectivity became a matter of great concern. Indeed it may grow into even greater concerns if advances in neurophysiology reveal that the apparent dualism between mind and matter can be resolved only when objective and subjective investigations can be synthesized. The methodology of science has proven to be adequate for understanding objective phenomena. The methodology of phenomenology promises to help in the understanding subjective phenomena.

---

[3] Smith, David Woodruff, "Phenomenology", *The Stanford Encyclopedia of Philosophy* (2013)

The methods of phenomenology[Smith, D.]

Classical:

(1) Description - Husserl (1859 –1938) and Merleau-Ponty (1908 –1961) described a type of experience just as we find it in our own (past) experience, and proposed phenomenology as a pure description of lived experience.

(2) Interpretation - Heidegger and his followers interpreted a type of experience by relating it to relevant features of context and spoke of hermeneutics, the art of interpretation in context, especially social and linguistic context (i.e., existence in this world).

(3) Analysis - In the end, all the classical phenomenologists practiced analysis of a type of experience, factoring out notable features for further elaboration.

Expanded:

(4) In a logico-semantic model of phenomenology, we specify the truth conditions for a type of thinking (e.g., I think that dogs chase cats) or the satisfaction conditions for a type of intention (e.g., I intend or will to jump that hurdle).

(5) In the experimental paradigm of cognitive neuroscience, we design empirical experiments that tend to confirm or refute aspects of experience (e.g., a brain scan shows electrochemical activity in a specific region of the brain thought to subserve a type of vision or

emotion or motor control). This style of "neurophenomenology" assumes that conscious experience is grounded in neural activity in embodied action in appropriate surroundings — mixing pure phenomenology with biological and physical science in a way that was not wholly congenial to traditional phenomenologists.

Mental Model

Many innovators, in the process of formulating their
theses, have developed a mental model. These were
not just examples of concrete thinking, but were
substitutes for experiments that could not be done
empirically. They were *metaphors* or *thought
experiments*. Plato conceived of abstract thinking as
shadows on the wall, Galileo imagined the effect of
falling bodies of varying weights, Newton explored the
aspects of gravity based on 1. falling apples 2. the
trajectory of a cannon ball shot with ever increasing
force, Freud imagined the workings of the mind in
hydrodynamic terms, Einstein envisioned the effects
of running at the speed of light. Feynman created
simple diagrams to represent the behavior of
subatomic particles. He also used a stylized
checkerboard to represent space-time.

These models were usually very simple, or based on
technology coexistent at the time. The ultimate
description of how the mind works was, and remains,
unknown. So far, it remains uncertain whether there is
even anything that could be called the mind. One
thing is certain, in all this - the vocabulary we all use,
in common, was developed out of a need to have an
expression to refer to a phenomenon that enough
people have experienced. The words chosen by
usage have undergone many changes, as do all
words in a living language. It seems that the most
productive way to gain information on the concept that
is expressed by the vocabulary is to find the earliest
form of the word and see how its meaning fits into its
use at the time[Heidegger]. The project introduced here
derives from the many gaps in meaning caused by

the adoption of words that were originated to signify ineffable phenomena, including nearly all abstract nouns. The toxic effect is not from the adoption but from the usurpation of meaning. We all accept the commonly used meanings in society to some degree, or the concept of meaning would be destroyed, as Wittgenstein implied in his thought experiment - *Beetle in a Box*. If this statement were extended *reductio ad absurdum*, perhaps even language itself would lose meaning.

In accommodation to this possibly harsh reality, we exist on a level of shared understanding. Many who, of necessity, share this mental space, may also share other more specialized spaces and share a vocabulary that economizes concepts in that sphere (doctors, lawyers, clergy, philosophers). The gap is well described:

> "The term 'philosophy' is used in two very different senses: one to describe a well-defined tradition of systematic and methodical inquiry; the other, which might be called 'folk-philosophy' or 'ethno-philosophy',... to describe the set of cultural variations on a range of beliefs about nature, the self, etc., which humans qua human cannot help but have." [Smith, J.]

He does not claim these senses to be hierarchical, but "a clash of provincialisms." It may be this clash which interferes with resolution of the mind-body problem. This effort is an attempt to find the elemental meaning of the words used in discussing the mind to encourage progress in understanding the terms and enhance the construction of an integrated concept.

Choosing a Model

The model proposed here should not be taken literally, but as a stylized way, i.e., a simplified way, deprived of non-essentials to improve clarity. This technique is not to hide details, but suspend them on representation to the mind, and to clarify speculation on how it works. It is called stylized to emphasize the absence of adornments, that seem to attach themselves in any dialectical analysis of words, and tend to euphemize meaning, either inflating it beyond its essence or flattening it with loss of essential aspects. Socrates witnessed the inflation of meaning in the Sophists, and Heidegger warned of flattening meaning in inauthentic usage:

> "Nevertheless, the ultimate business of philosophy is to preserve the force of the most elemental words in which Dasein expresses itself, and to keep common understanding from leveling them off to that unintelligibility which functions in turn as a source of pseudo-problems." [Heidegger]

It is hoped these trimmed down versions of honestly felt concepts will serve as guides to an acceptable formation of the concept of the mind.

Many of the adaptations of these terms over time seem superfluous to our use, but were developed in the service of entities who honestly were employed in the aid of their fellow beings. Just as we readapt these concepts to our use, it is hoped they also can trim the terms to essentials in their disciplines. In addition, when approaching a problem "theory laden", a technique must be used to unravel the "muddle". To date, the methods of phenomenology are some of the few reliable approaches available. "Wittgenstein came to conclude that his work had to be ultimately understood in terms of phenomenology." [Fernández]

Ideas too big for words

The word *mind* is derived from from the word *psyche*, as are *soul*, *spirit*, and *anima*. Psyche (Gk. *Psuche* life, soul) is translated into Latin as anima. Soul attained an ecclesiastical cachet in medieval times which transcribed the concept into an abstract self which was conceived as continuing through eternity. That notion existed in Plato, who felt things of the world are not real and subject to deterioration. He credited a secret society that promulgated that idea. It also has roots in Hindu philosophy, which has been modified by various denominations, but essentially is that part of the universe (sometimes personalized as a divine power, just as our concept attaches to God) that attaches to our physical being to aid in its spiritual development, then returns to rejoin its origin, as our souls are said to do. There were connections amongst Plato, the secret society and Vedic thinkers.[4] The nature of those connections is unclear; but evidences do exist in Platonic writings.

The word *Spirit*, derives from its latin meaning as breath or essence. It was a natural fit for soul. Most of these terms apply to the essence that makes the difference between a corpse and a body. The concept of life developed both as notion that explained the difference from death and as a term to refer to the act of living (longevity, span, persistence).

Just as *mind*, *soul*, *spirit* and *anima* are derived from from the word *psyche,* so is the word *psyche* derived from the body for which it is the animating principle. That body, including all forms of its animating

---

[4] Kurgan hypothesis. [STEVKO]

principle(s) is referred to objectively (when we speak of other bodies with their animating principles) as persons, characters, folks, individuals, and referred to objectively (when we speak of our own bodies with their animating principles) as the Self [5].

Self is the object of consciousness, just as other selves are the object of our consciousness. Yet, our own consciousness and its contents are our subjective material. This ability to look at (at least aspects of) ourselves is the basis of reflective thinking, which forms the basis of philosophical thinking.

Reflective thinking has more simply been referred to as thinking about thinking; yet that very simplified definition is not adequate to reveal how philosophy differs from something that goes on in our minds every time a new perception is processed and disquiets relevant memories. How does that become philosophy?

The first distinction that comes to mind is the quality of elevation, or, as the seekers of the sixties [6] referred

---

[5] Interestingly, when speaking of intentionality (the direction of attention, about-ness), subjectivity is about internal reality, and the subject is a thinking of feeling entity; objectivity is about external reality, and the object is that about which thinking or feeling is done. Paradoxically, the Self is the object of consciousness.

[6] Initially those involved in legitimate research on psychedelic drugs, e.g., Ken Kesey on the West Coast and Timothy Leary on the East Coast, subsequently fomenting the Psychedelic Revolution.

to *higher consciousness*. Not to get impeded by recreational referents, but to explore the difference between thinking and reflection, let us compare levels of thinking. A lowest level thought is an awareness of sense data that is processed by comparing it to other similar thoughts in memory that are previously processed sense data. A higher level thought began as a low level thought that has been processed, thereby increasing in complexity by associating characteristics of other low level thoughts; thereby creating a more complex notion. These more complex notions are stored in memory, and made available to lower level thoughts to form intermediate level thoughts and are also made available, on stimulation, to consciousness in progressive degrees to form the highest, usually abstract notions that can be reflected to other consciousnesses in what is called dialogue. At what level the distinction is made to call the thought an idea or a notion or even a concept becomes a topic for future reflection. The classification of levels is beyond the scope of this reflection; but seems to involve an ancillary issue of warranty, or how do we come to accept a concept as true.

Psychologically, these concepts are based on other concepts that may have birth in sense data, but have superimposed so many layers of reflection and association internally that we cannot find the bond to the sensory world and reify them as though they were tangible beings in a separate reality.

Appendix

Lexical definition
mental (adj.) O.E.D. - Of or relating to the mind
archaeology (n.) O.E.D.- The study of human history
and prehistory through the excavation of sites and the
analysis of artifacts and other physical remains.
archaeology (n.) M.W. - a science that deals with past
human life and activities by   studying the bones,
tools, etc., of ancient people.
archaeology (full definition) M.W. - 1: the scientific
study of material remains (as fossil   relics,
artifacts, and monuments) of past human life and
activities
        2: remains of the culture of a people :
antiquities
Dasein - a fundamental concept of being-in-the-
worldness, worldliness expressed:
        in the existential philosophy [Heidegger],
particularly in his magnum opus   Being and
Time.
        in the Taoist philosophy of Zhuangzi as
expressed by Okakura Kakuzo's 1906 *The Book of
Tea,* Duffield & Company to describe
concept of (*das-in-der-Welt-sein*)

Etymology
Early 17th century from modern Latin *archaeologia* (in
the sense 'ancient history'):
from Greek *arkhaiologia* 'ancient history':
from *arkhaios* 'ancient' (see archaeo-).
Mid 19th century (the current sense 'study of the past
as informed by artifacts)

O.E.D.

Considering all lexical definitions and etymology, the central issue seems to revolve around "physical remains," commonly called *artifacts*. In its lexical meaning, "a thing fabricated (as opposed to one that occurs naturally)."

Bibliography

Benjamin, Walter, *Gesammelte Schriften*, IV, 400–401, written
  ca. 1932; published   1991.
Binford, Lewis R. *In pursuit of the future.* 1986.
  in Meltzer, David J.; Fowler, Donald D., and Sabloff,
Jeremy A., editors.
  American Archaeology past and future. Washington,
  D.C.: Smithson Institution Press.
Ety. Dictionary of Etymology
Fernández, J. R., *Wittgenstein's phenomenology and
  Wittgenstein's phenomenological relevance,* POLISH
  JOURNAL OF PHILOSOPHY Vol. III, No. 2 (Fall 2009),
  17-27.
Freud Museum London *Freud and Archaeology*
Foucault, M., *Archeology of Knowledge*
Gutting, Gary, from *Archaeology to Genealogy* in"Michel
Foucault", The Stanford Encyclopedia of Philosophy (Winter
  2014 Edition), Edward N. Zalta (ed.)
Heidegger, M., *Being and Time*, (Macquarrie tr.) p.262
Jung, C. G., *Man and his Symbols* (London 1978)
Larsen, Steen F., *Remembering and the Archaeology Metaphor,*
  Metaphor and Symbolic Activity, Volume 2, Issue 3, 1987
M.W. Merriam-Webster Dictionary
O.E.D Oxford English Dictionary
Panksepp, J., and Biven, L., Norton Series on Interpersonal
  Neurobiology *The Archaeology of Mind:
  NEUROEVOLUTIONARY ORIGINS OF HUMAN
  EMOTIONS*
Reigl, A., *Historische Grammatik der bildenden Künste
  (Historical grammar of the visual arts).*
Smith, David Woodruff, "Phenomenology", *The Stanford
  Encyclopedia of Philosophy* (2013)
Smith, Justin E. H. *A Plea for Folk-Philosophy,* An Archive of
  Philosophy, News, Notes, and Academic Work in
  Progress.
Society for American Archaeology
Spiegelberg, H., *The Phenomenological Movement.*
Stevko, R. *Before Philosophy.*
Varela, F. J., Thompson, Evan T., and Rosch, Eleanor. *The
  Embodied Mind: Cognitive Science and Human
  Experience.* (1991). Cambridge, MA: The MIT Press.
Varela, F.J., *Neurophenomenology: a methodological remedy for
  the hard problem,* Journal of Consciousness Studies,
  Volume 3, Number 4, 1996

Richard Stevko was born in the megalopolis of Bost-Wash and raised on the banks of the Aquashicola Creek. The duality of these influences lent credence and even provided a paradigm for understanding the city-country, sophisticated-innocent and many other aspects of Self we all need to engage. A retired healer and teacher, he lives and writes near the banks of the Scantic River.

www.ingramcontent.com/pod-product-compliance
Lightning Source LLC
Chambersburg PA
CBHW050354290526
45785CB00006B/2774